# VALIANT
# AIR COMMAND

# VALIANT
# AIR COMMAND

**Osprey Colour Series**

photography
Norman Pealing

commentary
Mike Savage

Published in 1990 by Osprey Publishing Limited
59 Grosvenor Street, London W1X 9DA

Photographs © Norman Pealing 1990

Commentary © Mike Savage 1990

British Library Cataloguing in Publication Data

Pealing, Norman
    Valiant Air Command.
    1. Air displays
    I. Title
    629.13'074

    ISBN 0-85045-954-0

Editor Dennis Baldry
Designed by Simon Ray-Hills
Printed in Hong Kong

**Front cover** Leader of the pack: Steve Sevier, in 'MD' Cashion's immaculate Beech C-45, holds formation for the benefit of Norman Pealing's camera as an amazing variety of other Valiant Air Command machines (all of which are featured within this book) form up behind

**Title pages** Not many of us can boast our very own anti-submarine aircraft, but Dave Brady can—and does! Here he taxies out at Tico in preparation for a 'bombing run'. This particular Grumman Tracker was built in 1952 and is powered by a pair of Wright R-1820 Cyclone nine-cylinder radial engines of 1525 hp each

**Right** John Silberman's as-new looking Fouga CM-170 Magister high up near Tico and wearing the livery of the only Air Force to use these twin jets operationally, that of Israel. Originally developed from the Fouga Cyclone, a powered glider with one tiny jet mounted on top of its fuselage and exhausting through the butterfly tail, the Magister is an extremely successful trainer, some 191 examples of which remain in service with the French Air Force. Power comes from two Turboméca Marboré 880-pound thrust turbojets giving a maximum speed of just over 400 mph, a ceiling of 36,000 feet and the aircraft has a range approaching 500 miles

# Introduction

A young organization, the Valiant Air Command was started only in 1977 by a very dedicated group of private individuals—with just two warbirds! Since that time, it has grown from its original 12 members to an international membership with over 350 historic military aircraft.

Based at Titusville, Florida—just across the Indian river from Cape Canaveral—the VAC is recognized as an educational 'Flying Museum' and has an earnest belief that the true history of its warbirds can only be expressed when the aircraft are flown for all to see and admire. This happens at least annually and the Spring three-day display is the one that brings the hordes!

With the basic goal of finding and preserving the historic military aircraft that have done so much to establish and preserve our peace, the VAC is very much a part of America's national aviation heritage. To this end a permanent museum is being built on the perimeter of the 'Space Center Executive Airport', as Titusville is properly known. This multi-million dollar project—all from private funds—will become the focal point of the VAC's restoration projects— as well as a chronicle of US military aviation through the ages. At the moment these proceed in rather less spacious surroundings.

Membership of the VAC is open to anyone who is interested—you don't have to own an aircraft, be a pilot or even an aircraft engineer, just have a keen interest in warbird history. The VAC welcomes people of all walks of life who share just one desire—to see that these aircraft, and the memory of the men and women who flew them and serviced them, is preserved for future generations.

And if it rains, which the VAC hardly ever allows? The magnificent Spaceport Museum is but a ride way, as is Disneyworld, just up the road towards Miami at Orlando.

For more, search these pages and contact:

Valiant Air Command
Operations Officer
6600 Tico Road
Titusville, Florida 32780
(305) 268–1941

# The authors

NORMAN PEALING, FRPS, began taking pictures before he entered the Royal Air Force in 1958, but his photographic portfolio was not allowed to expand into aviation subjects in the days when RAF Marham and Wittering were stuffed full of Valiant nuclear bombers.

In 1965 he joined the British Aircraft Corporation (BAC), and began making sales/publicity films to promote all the company's products, which included guided weapons, satellites, military and civil aircraft. He attended many first flights and took part in the demonstration tours of the One-Eleven and Concorde airliners.

In 1983 he chose to leave what had become the Weybridge Division of British Aerospace (BAe) to form his own company at Fairoaks Airport in Surrey. The Aviation Film Company (AFC), specializes in aviation photography and film/video production for advertising, sales support, public relations, publishing, and television requirements.

The photographs in VALIANT AIR COMMAND were all taken with Hasselblad cameras and lenses, loaded with Ektachrome EPN 100 roll film.

MIKE SAVAGE is Vice President PR and Promotions for Saab Aircraft International Limited, dealing with the 340 and 2000 regional airliners in all regions except North America and Canada.

He began his aviation career 'sometime in the fifties', he recalls, as a student of aircraft engineering at the de Havilland Technical School in Hatfield, Hertfordshire. A commission in the Royal Air Force followed, during which he was selected for the first (and probably the last) 'all-through' jet training course at RAF Syerston in Nottinghamshire. After leaving the RAF, he fell into the employ of Handley Page Limited, where he helped in marketing the Dart Herald airliner and promoting the Victor V-bomber.

Mike Savage has been involved in public relations and marketing ever since, having worked for the British Hovercraft Corporation (where he tried unsuccessfully to sell hovercraft to the Indian Coast Guard); the British Aircraft Corporation where he was responsible for the initial overseas publicity of the BAC One-Eleven short-range airliner, and later became PR Manager for BAC's Commercial Aircraft Division during the development and proving trials for Concorde in 1972–6 and its early airline service in 1976–8; and spent six years in the Arabian Gulf, mostly with Gulf Air, until he returned to the UK and joined Saab Aircraft International in 1984.

# Acknowledgements

This is always the most difficult part of any book to write, since with no malice aforethought, someone always gets left out, but here goes:

First, Bill Noriega, the VAC 'Boss' and Tico ATC maestro; Bob James, his most able Operations Director; Jim Hawkins, who has the unenviable task of PR and media handling; Kevin Quinlan, who so ably organizes and runs the annual VAC auction that brings in such vital extra funds, and all the other dedicated men and women without whom the Valiant Air Command would grind to a halt.

Then all the pilots and groundcrews who contribute so much to an outstanding display—some of the more venerable warbirds need anything up to 20 hours' servicing for each hour in the air! Invidious though it is to single out just a few aviators and not all, special thanks to 'Robbie' Robinson and Dale Krebsbach with their B-25 *Chapter XI*; Steve Sevier, who with owner 'MD' Cashion flies the cover picture Navy C-45; Mike Brady, ever-willing to fly his immaculate T-34 as either photo-ship or to pose as willing subject; Dr John Parsons, VAC 1989's most accomplished T-34 Leader and the late-lamented Walter Meyer, another unstinting Mentor owner-pilot whose aircraft was always available for air-to-air photography.

As well, all those ever-patient warbird owners, pilots and servicing crews who were always happy not only to speak into a tape recorder at all the most inconvenient times and places, but also really did send on promised information.

Assistant editor Cathy Lowne had the unenviable task of transforming this ink slinger's incoherent commentary into readable text. Many thanks!

A plaudit for the noble editor, Dennis Baldry, whose driving between the Space Shuttle Inn and the Valiant Air Command Airshow was something of a cross between a lap in the Indy 500 and being stuck in the middle of a demolition derby. We pledge that all proceeds from this volume will go towards driving lessons in preparation for his next stint at the wheel en route to some other US warbirds show—Dennis, we're all too young to die yet!

# Contents

One of the few really affordable warbirds, the Cessna L-19 is a lot of fun to fly. With a top speed of 100 mph, it will fly at 45 and take off in 300 feet. Power comes from a Continental 0470−11 engine of 213 hp. Some 3431 Cessna 'Bird Dogs' were built and the first came off the production line in December 1950, right in the middle of the Korean war. They served as spotters, light transports, trainers (with the French Air Force in this role, too) and—like this one—as aggressors, carrying light bombs beneath the wings. Featuring a fixed-pitch prop, the L-19 is a touch thirsty at up to 11 gallons per hour

# T-28 Trojan: the affordable warbird?

**Left** Originally, the North American T-28 Trojan was powered by an 800 hp R-1300 Wright Cyclone air cooled radial engine, but the later T-28D version, the last to be built, has a 1425 hp Wright R-1820–56A motor. This type is the most commonly flown today

**Below** This US Navy T-28C shows off its arrestor hook; its retraction mechanism and structural strengthening increased the maximum weight of the 'C' to 8500 pounds and overall performance suffered: its service ceiling came down to 35,500 feet; its climb rate fell to 3500 feet/min; its top speed to only 343 mph and range to 860 miles. Only four examples of this particular mark are known to exist

**Left** North American's T-28 Trojan was designed as a basic trainer to replace AT-6s serving with the USAF. It flew for the first time in 1949 and entered production the following year. In all, nearly 2000 Trojans of all marks were built up until 1957. Note the excellent view for both occupants and the characteristic black paint stripe to coincide with exhaust stain as it follows the airflow over the wing

**Left** The Trojan's specification stated that it should emulate the performance and flight characteristics of jet aircraft and a speed brake was installed on all T-28s from the 'B' model onwards. Although the initial prototypes—three were built—were taildraggers, a tricycle undercarriage also became standard. The first of these prototypes (which also featured a speed brake, to be deleted from initial production aircraft) was the XBT-28 which flew on 26 September 1949

It was during 1947 that the US Air Force issued a specification to the American industry for a new trainer to replace the Texan. It had to be an all-metal, low-winged aircraft with tandem seating for both instructor and student. The engine for the new trainer would be Government

Furnished Equipment, the chosen powerplant being the 800 hp R-1300 Wright Cyclone and a two-bladed Aero Products propeller.

This peel-away shot shows off the T-28's smooth, uncluttered lines— little altered from 'Day One', the sure sign of a sound design. A T-28B1, it differs from the 'A' model in having a larger, more powerful engine, three-bladed propeller, speed brake and a smaller nosewheel. It also introduced the two-section sliding bubble canopy that subsequently became standard

Two classic warbirds pose together near Tico in the evening sun—the big Grumman Avenger torpedo bomber and a North American T-28 Trojan. While the Avenger is indeed a rare bird, whole flocks of T-28s can be seen flying in the US

This sprightly 'rotate' by a pair of Trojans at the VAC Spring Airshow is typical. And another half-dozen or more were already airborne. This big trainer, which dwarves its AT-6 precursor, is a popular mount for preservation buffs in North America, but is almost unheard of elsewhere

**Above** As a trainer from both terra firma and seaborne lumps of pitching steel, the Trojan's 'boots' had to be strong. The nosewheel retracts into a well on the underside of the fuselage and the two main landing gear members—each equipped with Goodyear disc brakes—retract inward into wells located on the underside of the wing and fuselage. As well as being steerable, the nosewheel strut carries a movable taxi light to assist the night operations

**Right** The tiny nosewheel of the North American T-28B—and later versions— runs at a much higher pressure than the fatter one on the 'A'. This helps the aircraft to 'stick down' much better on touchdown

**Below** Preparing for take-off, this T-28's Wright R-1820—56S crackles into life, turning its ten foot, one inch diameter Hamilton Standard three-bladed propeller. Early on in the Trojan's life, its engine was installed with visible droop, such were increases in power from the original 800 hp to 1425

**Right** Anyone for tennis? A novel way of keeping bugs and moisture out of your T-28 exhaust stacks. History has yet to record just how far these would go if you forgot to remove them before pressing the button. It would certainly be game, set and match!

Time for reflection. The distant sun glistens on the grey paintwork of this Navy North American T-28 Trojan as the first day of the VAC's three-day event draws to a close

**Left** A row of Tico Trojans awaits its turn to perform in the warm Florida air. The nearest one is a T-28A—it has two exhaust stacks as opposed to the three on later models. It was the T-28A that was eventually modified into the 'O' for light attack in Vietnam, and also in the Congo where multi-million dollar jets proved impractical

**Right** The T-28A Trojan—with its fat nosewheel—also sported the longer oil cooler intake right up to the lip of the cowling. Atop the cowling is the carburettor air intake and to the right of this Trojan's nose art can be seen the open cooling gill flap. From any angle, the Trojan looks a workmanlike piece of kit

**Right** Airbrush artistry. A pugilistic 'Danny Boy' with Anglo-Irish overtones graces this T-28 nose

The T-28 represented a major improvement in training aircraft and proved to be very popular with both flight and groundcrews for its excellent flight characteristics and ease of maintenance. Its only initial drawback was its engine, the original 800 hp unit making it underpowered, although this was a deliberate ploy to give the Trojan the 'feel' of an early jet aircraft. The take-off run was long and sluggish, especially on a hot day, and this sluggishness persisted in the air. The considerably more powerful motors later fitted solved the problem

# Class act: T-34 Mentor

**Left** Dave Marco's Navy Beech T-34 Mentor sports tip tanks—
when flying 'solo' Dave is seldom separated from his furry friend! Production of
the Navy T-34B ended in October 1957, after 423 had been built. Not only is
the Turbine Mentor (powered by a Pratt & Whitney of Canada PT6A-25
turboprop de-rated to 400 hp) still operating with the US Navy, but 19 have
recently been built from new to account for attrition

**Below** Two of the 350 Beech T-34As that were produced for the USAF
formate on Dave Marco's 'B' model. T-34s are now very much a part of the
warbird community and are represented by the T-34 Association which is
dedicated to the professional flying of these superb trainers, originally based on
the Beech Bonanza

**Left** Two light grey 'Air Force' T-34s warm up at Tico. With a span of 32 feet eight inches and a length of 25 feet nine inches, the T-34 is a roomy aircraft grossing at 3000 pounds. It had 50 US gallons of usable fuel and burns it at 15·5 gph. At 165 knots this gives a range of about 350 miles. Fully aerobatic, its G limits are + 6 and − 3

**Above** the late great Walter Meyer—a leading member of the T-34 Association and much-missed warbird pilot—flying one of only ten T-34s armed in anger (to fight in Honduras) en route to his home in Beaumont, Texas, after the 1988 VAC show. His mount featured machine guns in the wings, hard-points and genuine (patched over) bullet holes in the tail from random small arms fire from the ground

**Inset** A gaggle of gurgling T-34s taxi out for a formation take-off followed by some tight, well-disciplined close flying. A lot of Mentors attend US warbird displays—especially Tico—and in 1987 at Oshkosh the ultimate T-34 formation flew by: 34 T-34s

Five shiny yellow T-34s in a neater 'vic' than this picture shows. Soon after Charlie Nogle and Earle Parks formed the T-34 Association, they devised a formation training programme to take the 'hair' out of 'hairy' flying at warbird displays. Along with a manual, Wingman and Leader pilot designations were devised and this system has led to T-34 pilots being in the forefront of professionalism and safety

**Left** A Canadian visitor to VAC in a Canadian Beech Mentor in echelon with a US Navy companion high over Florida. In 1956 the Canadians needed a replacement for both the Chipmunk and Harvard and in a joint venture built 150 'north of the border', 25 for themselves and the rest for US use. In the event these 25 were only in service with the RCAF for 18 months, after which they were sold to Turkey

**Below left** Just a microsecond after the shutter closed, the wingman pulled into line—isn't it always the way when you run out of film? The view from the almost 'bubble' canopy is excellent and the interior roomy—roomy enough for Ramona Cox in her wedding gown when she and fellow pilot Kris married when airborne in a T-34 some years ago!

**Right** Four key members of the T-34 Association formate on another Mentor photo-ship. Leader is Dr John Parsons, an orthodontist from San Antonio; then Earl Arrowood with his unusually 'civil' Mentor (Earl sells, charters and leases aircraft in Gainesville, Georgia); Mike Brady, the 'boss' of leading regional airline Northwest Airlink, in his 1988 Oshkosh 'best in show' T-34 which features a big 335 hp Continental IO-520BA and better avionics than Concorde, and lastly Dave Marco in the tip-tanked Navy T-34. Dave runs his own company selling ophthalmic equipment out of Jacksonville. Get into line Mr Brady, Sir!

Here's proof that Mr Brady does get into line—and stays there for a very long time! But there is no truth in the rumour that this is a dawn shot! This is surely a superb example of professional airmanship and the leader's absolute confidence in his companions. Remember, these aviators are 'amateurs' in the truest sense of the word

# Texan variations

**Left** Who has never heard of the 'Harvard', as it was known in RAF service? Arguably the best known trainer ever—after the Tiger Moth, maybe—15,000 North American AT-6 Texans were built between 1940 and 1951. It was the USAF's basic and advanced trainer right up to 1956 and with the tips of its two-bladed prop frequently going supersonic the din is unmistakable

**Below** More than 50,000 USAF and another 40,000 US Navy and Marine student pilots have sat in AT-6 and SJN (Navy version) 'greenhouse' cockpits like this—plus countless more from 34 nations. AT-6s still serve with several Third World air forces and many are in the careful hands of warbird buffs, as evidenced by those at the Valiant Air Command show at Tico

**Above** As a pair of AT-6s strafe the 'Yellow Peril', a somewhat incongrous collection of ironmongery awaits below! At the VAC annual air display, the USAF and Marine Corps can always be relied upon to put on a fine show with the latest in earth-shattering 'heavy metal'

**Left** Texans at Tico. The roar of 550 hp P & W R-1340—49 Wasp nine-cylinder radials at AT-6s taxi out prior to beating up the baddies. Not only did Texans see service in Korea as humble but valuable spotters, they also saw combat duty in Java during the Pacific War, armed with both 0·30 calibre guns and bombs

37

**Left** The US Navy version of the AT-6 was designated SJN but was, to all intents and purposes, the same aeroplane. Both variants cruise at 170 mph at 5000 feet and have a range of 750 miles. Maximum take-off weight is 5550 pounds. In addition to Australia (where the type was known as the Wirraway), AT-6s were licence-built in Sweden and Canada

**Below** Derived from the earlier North American BT-9 trainer of 1935 vintage, the AT-6 kept its predecessor's general lines, but was greatly improved. In particular, the fixed undercarriage was changed for this widely-spaced retracting gear, placed well forward. Both characteristics were much appreciated by students of the throttle-bending persuasion during ground manoeuvres!

With a lot of wing area, the AT-6 is not only agile, but is a fine aerobatic mount. No less than 5000 Harvards served the RAF with distinction and the last British pilot qualified on the type on 22 March 1955

The Texan's outer wing panels are attached in the same way as those on the C-47—rows of bolts joining mating flanges, the resulting ridge being faired over with a top and bottom cover plate. In this view the starboard single exhaust and neat undercarriage retraction arrangement are shown to advantage

**Right** The original Wirraway—it means 'Challenge' in the Aborigine tongue—was an AT-6 built in Melbourne, Australia, by the Commonwealth Aircraft Corporation under North American licence. It was by far the most famous Australian-built aircraft of World War 2

**Below** Powered by a geared 600 hp P & W R-1340, the Wirraway features a split exhaust system with the engine surrounded by an efficient NACA (now NASA) cowling. A three-bladed variable-pitch constant speed propeller is fitted to this advanced trainer, also pressed into front-line service as a fighter

**Left** This 'Oz' Navy Wirraway is a CA.20. The Wirraway first went into Australian military service in July 1939 with the RAAF as an advanced trainer, but also flew as a stop-gap fighter with distinction in both Malaya and the South West Pacific

**Below** The distinctive Kangaroo roundel on this early Wirraway shows up clearly on the Australian Navy grey background. For operations against the Japanese, the 'red rat', as the leaping marsupial was rudely dubbed, was often deleted. This was because in the heat of a battle, a Wirraway could be mistaken for a *Zero*, and a plain white roundel with a blue circumference made it easier not to shoot down your 'cobber' by mistake. North American's single-seat fighter version of the AT-6, the P-64, reposes in the background

**Overleaf** Anyone with around $200,000 to spare at Tico could have purchased this lovely P-64 (company designation NA-50), resplendent in USAAC livery. One of a mere 13 of the type ever built, this neat 'razorback' version of the AT-6 series caused a good deal of head-scratching amongst enthusiasts

**Left** Beech C-45 leads the pack, powered by two 450 hp P & W R-985s. Maximum all-up weight is 9300 pounds and the C-45 can reach 219 mph. Normal cruising speed is 150 mph at 8000 feet, using 45 per cent power. With a service ceiling of 18,200 feet, a range of 1140 miles can be achieved

**Overleaf** A fine warbird echelon— Steve Sevier flies the immaculate Navy Beech C-45 ahead of an AT-6, a BT-13 (which the AT-6 replaced as advanced trainer) a P.149 and an Me 208. A derivative of the highly popular Beech 18 pre-war light transport, the C-45 was produced between 1939 and 1945 in four versions: the AT-7 'Navigator' navigational trainer; AT-11 'Kansas' bombing and gunnery trainer (also used for navigator training) and N-2 for aerial photography and mapping, as well as the basic transport

A wide-chord, low-aspect ratio wing is a feature of the Beech C-45. Such was the popularity of this versatile machine that during the 1950s Beech completely rebuilt 900, issued them with new serial numbers and pressed them into service as C-45Gs and C-45Hs. Many are still flying today and at least one version—that by Volpar Inc—was used as an executive transport, with an extended nose, turboprops, updated avionics and tricycle undercarriage

# 'Bad guys'

**Left** You don't have to be drunk to paint a warbird spinner—but it does help! Close-up of the spinner, propeller and cowling on Phil Appelquist's fascinating French-built Me 208. It certainly attracts even the doziest of flight-line jay walkers to the fact that something's turning and it could just bite

**Below** Phil Appelquist's rare Nord Aviation-built Messerschmitt Me 208 has been re-engined with an IGSO 450 hp motor replacing the original 230 hp Renault unit. So carefully has Phil remodelled the engine cowling that not even Willy Messerschmitt would know the difference. There is an extraordinary amount of wing dihedral

**Overleaf** Three of the Me 208s built by Nord under German occupation during World War 2 were brought into the US in 1965—this one is the only survivor. One crashed and the other was rendered down for spares. With its new powerplant, this example cruises at 175 mph and will reach 250. Fond of fuel, the IGSO 540 engine burns 14 gallons per hour at cruise power and over double that amount flat out. Before reaching North America, Phil Appelquist's Me 208 flew with the French Air Force, having been re-licensed in 1947. This aircraft was the 107th to be produced

**Below** An elegant aircraft from any angle, the Me 208 was originally designed as a roomy four-place tourer. For its day the tricycle undercarriage was a novel feature. This particular example, flying over lowlands close to Tico, was built in 1943—but was still in its jigs in the German-held Nord Aviation factory in France when it was liberated by the Allies. In order to frustrate their enemy masters, aircraft built in France for the Germans took a strangely long time to complete and often fell apart in the air through minor oversights, such as understrength wing bolts!

Not all replicas are fun, but this one certainly is! It is a fairly close approximation of a Junkers CL.1 and was produced from a Snow S-2A crop duster in 1960. Note the thick Clark Y end-plated wing and low ground angle

**Left** The rear hopper compartment of the original Snow S-2A crop duster donor airframe makes an ideal gunner's position. The fundamental windscreen 'roll-over' arch is a prominent feature—so far nobody has found out if it works! But what a Concours finish on this fun Junkers

**Below** Non-standard power for the replica Junkers CL.1 comes from a Continental W-670 of 240 hp. It is a converted Sherman tank engine, although in the air the Junkers sounds more like a rather tired levitating loom. The controls are delightfully basic—and could that be the Red Baron's helmet on the coaming?

**Right** Italian jobs, but German built. A pair of Focke Wulf-built Piaggio P.149s—two of the (appropriately) 190 produced by this company in the 1950s

**Below** The Piaggio P.149 was developed from the earlier taildragger P.148 and this equally elegant aircraft was put into service with the *Aeronautica Militare Italia* in 1952

**Below** An exercise in camouflage as a Focke Wulf-built Piaggio P.149 cruises low over the flatlands near Tico. The somewhat faded 'dayglo' rudder, nose and wingtips need no explanation!

**Right** Surely all the joys of flying are summed up in this triple P.149 tailchase in perfect Florida weather. In all, 262 Piaggio P.149s were built and this uprated tricycle undercarriaged P.148 came into being in 1953

**Left** Three Fuji-built Beech T-34s taxi out at Tico to join the baddies for a VAC set-piece attack 'somewhere in the Pacific'. Several of these interesting four-seat derivatives fly on the American airshow scene and are useful additions to the stocks of 'homebuilt' *Zeros, Kates* and *Vals*

**Below** Built under licence from Beechcraft by Fuji Industries in Japan, the T-34 was produced in four separate versions. This example is a four-seater (three of the variants were configured in this way and one, the LM-2 *Nikko*, had an optional fifth seat) and in this shot the extra-wide fuselage shows up. Power is a 340 hp Lycoming IGSO-480-A1F6 engine

If you want an instant *Val* (Aichi D3A) for your Florida Pearl Harbor re-enactment, simple. Just take a spare BT-13, generously baste with Sake, and bingo, here it is, complete with 551-pound centreline bomb! In April 1942, highly skilled *Val* pilots demonstrated bombing accuracies of 80 per cent-plus by sinking the British carrier *Hermes* and heavy cruisers *Cornwall* and *Dorsetshire*

From 1940 until 1943, the standard US basic trainer was the Consolidated Vultee BT-13. Although 11,537 were built, it is quite rare today, but this example and several others can be seen flying with the VAC at Tico. These trainers introduced students not only to high-powered Pratt & Whitney and Wright engines, but to two-way radio and instrument flying as well. Known as the Vultee Valiant, the BT-13 (and BT-15) continued in service as late as 1950

**Above** Another ersatz *Val* taxies out at Tico on a Yank-zapping mission — only to be downed by a Corsair. Crime never did pay. Extremely strong and manoeuvrable, Aichi D3As made effective dogfighters with two wing-mounted 7·7 mm guns and another pivoted in the rear cockpit. In addition to the centreline bomb, two more 66-pounders could be carried under the wings

**Right** At airshows west of Okinawa — or east of Honolulu — the *Tora, Tora, Tora, Zeros* always have to lose. Wonder why? Here at Tico, Roy Stafford's Corsair F4U-1 is about to 'zap' an intruding North American 'intruder' masquerading as a 'baddy'. This particular Corsair served with both the Marine Corps and the US Navy and, according to its log book, was flown in World War 2 by Corsair ace Robert Hanson

# 'Seabirds'

**Left** The Corsair's characteristic gull-wing served two important purposes — apart from adding to the fine lines of this big fighter. It maintained an acceptably short main gear and ensured propeller clearance. This one is the only known F4U-1 (although its name plate erroneously calls it an F4U-2), serial number 7995, and is owned by Roy Stafford, from Jacksonville, Florida

**Below** A formidable Navy and Marine Fighter, the Chance Vought Corsair was considered by some pilots to be a better all-round war machine than the P-51. Its main undercarriage wheels rotate through 90 degrees for retraction and the tailwheel strut was lengthened early in the Corsair's history to counter a nasty and potentially lethal tendency. Previously, the angle of attack on carrier approach was so high for the approved three-pointer that, should the aircraft bounce on arrival, missing all wires, it would stall, drop a wing and hit either the 'island' or parked aircraft, or at best, go over the side. The new rear strut was appropriately called an 'incidence eliminator'!

**Below** Early Corsairs—this unique F4U-1 was completed on 30 September 1943, and still has less than 800 airframe hours—did not have the familiar 'bubble' canopy fitted to help improve forward vision over the long nose—the pilot's seat was also raised an extra six inches. Note the tiny bulge on the top of this canopy to accommodate the rear-view mirror. It is alleged that a novel feature of the Corsair was that it could be flown with the pilot standing. Apparently, the foot rests could slide away, thus allowing the pilot to stand in the belly of the aircraft. The control column was canted and could disappear into the lower instrument panel

**Right** Powered by a big P & W R-2800 radial, this Corsair will have a top speed of more than 300 knots. 'Will have' because it had just landed after its very first flight after a six-year rebuild and was prepared specially to appear at the VAC's 1989 airshow! Known as the '2000 dollar investment', Harry Done—who bought this F4U-1 from a lady who had acquired it surplus from Ogden, Utah, after the war—offered it to the Marine Corps for a museum at this price, but they backed out. Harry really wanted a helicopter. He subsequently got it into flying shape, but badly damaged it (but fortunately not himself) when it had a landing gear mishap upon touchdown on a salt lake. The wings, in particular, were a mess. This is when present owner Roy Stafford came along . . .

As the Avenger taxies out, the rear ball turret is clearly visible, as are the retracting bomb-bay doors—long enough to accommodate torpedoes. As well as dropping these weapons, the TBM-3E could carry 2000 pounds of iron bombs and be used for low-level attack or as a long-range scout. This one was built in March 1945, serial number 85794, and has just 1950 airframe hours

As the Grumman Avenger 'cleans up' after take-off, its considerable bulk becomes evident. It has an empty weight of 10,500 pounds and 'maxes out' at 18,500. Its owner, 'Coke' Stewart who hails from Georgia, says that his mount can carry seven passengers, each with a 100-pound baggage allowance, take on board 1000 pounds of tools and spares, be filled up to the brim with fuel and *still* be 6000 pounds under max gross!

A surprisingly elegant aircraft in flight, the Grumman TBM-3E is powered by a
Wright Cyclone 2600-20 of 1900 hp. This gives a never-exceed speed of
362 mph; a military cruise of 267 mph and a maximum consumption of 125
gallons per hour. Its armament comprises three 0·50 calibre and one 0·30 calibre
machine guns and eight five-inch rockets under each wing. A far cry from
owner 'Coke' Stewart's Korean mount — a Republic F-84, rudely but aptly
nicknamed 'the ground-hogging whore'

**Above** This TBM-3E Avenger
served aboard the USS *Yorktown*
(CV-10) from 16 July 1945 with
torpedo squadron VT-88. It has a
documented history of 11 combat
missions over Japanese mainland
targets. On 15 August 1945—the
day the war in Japan ended—George
Foot was flying this bomber with a
2000-pound bomb load, and heading
for a power plant. As he was directly
over the Imperial Palace in Tokyo, he
got the following radio call: *'The war
is over. Drop your bombs in the ocean
and come back and land!'*

**Right** High off the ground on its
long-oleo carrier deck landing gear,
'Coke' Stewart's TBM-3E Grumman
Avenger waits its turn on the flight-
line at Tico. This particular example
bears the name 'Lt George Bush' after
the Avenger the current President
flew during his wartime service in the
Pacific. He was shot down and his
two crewmen, Jack Delaney and Ted
White, perished. The paint scheme is
that of Lt Bush's squadron VTS-1
aboard the USS *San Jacinto*

**Above** With wings folded as if to guard against physical violence, the Grumman S-2A Tracker approaches Tico's flight-line after its slot in the VAC display. The ingenious folding mechanism ensures that the port wing parks in front of the starboard one, cutting down the carrier-borne hangarage needed to about one third of the Tracker's wingspan

**Right** Grumman—renowned for its design and development of naval aircraft—produced a potent submarine hunter/killer in the Tracker. It was tough, fast for its time (287 mph at 5000 feet) and could carry a 4810 pound weapons load. Maximum ceiling is 23,000 feet and the S-2A, with its four-man crew can fly for 900 miles. Its snub nose endows superb forward vision and the enormous fin area greatly assists engine-out handling. Nearly 1000 Trackers of differing marks were built and many survive to this day. In Canada and France, a turboprop powered version, the Conair Firecat, serves in the fire-fighting role

# Electra

**Left** An exercise in sweat and elbow grease. The shiny polished aluminium of Lou Hilton's beautiful Lockheed 12A Electra gleams on the VAC flight-line. A production run of 149 Electras in several variants, differing only in minor detail, found plenty of overseas customers, as well as those in the US where Northwest Airlines was the first to introduce the new airliner

**Below** The Lockheed 14 Super Electra was developed from the smaller 12A, and it was through a door like this that Neville Chamberlain disembarked from one of the larger aircraft, operated by British Airways Limited, when it landed at Heston on 24 September 1939. But a few weeks later, 'Peace in our time' had a hollow ring. With the onset of war, a further development of the 14 became the Lockheed Hudson, so familiar to Coastal Command crews of the RAF

The much sleeker Lockheed 12A Electra flies in formation with a Beech AT-11 and a Navy Beech C-45. These broadly similar twin-finned aircraft set new standards of luxury air travel (the AT-11 and C-45 in their original Beech 18 form) before the war. Lockheed Electras also broke several records and it was during an attempted round-the-world flight in one that Amelia Earhart was lost in the Pacific

The Lockheed Electra was developed in 1933 as the company's response to the Boeing 247, but Lockheed's engineers had to contend with a series of problems as it was their first all-metal aircraft. The difficulties having been overcome, the prototype made its first flight on 23 February 1934. Carrying the same number of passengers as the 247, the Electra was not only faster, but had better range and ceiling—and it was cheaper. It was, in fact, the lowest-priced aircraft in its class in the market and it was a commercial success from the start

Although designed around the same time as the Beech 18, and to a similar specification, the Lockheed 12A is altogether a slimmer, more graceful airliner. Powered by P & W R-985s, it carries eight passengers with a ninth in the copilot's seat. This one, wearing RAF roundels, was attached to the VIP Flight at Hendon in North London

# Bomber stream

**Below** This Beech AT-11 is owned by Lou Hilton, who flies it with John Hokanson, both from Palm Beach, Florida. In its training role of bombardier and navigator/trainer (note the Plexiglass dome atop the mid-fuselage), the AT-11's two 450 hp P & W R-985 Wasps give it a top speed of 215 mph and a ceiling of 24,500 feet. A creditable 745 miles can be covered at a 160 mph cruise speed. All-up weight is 7850 pounds

**Left** The Norden gunsight was a major breakthrough for World War 2 bombardiers and was top secret. For training bomb aimers in both the US Army Air Corps and Navy, the Beech 18 was adapted into this AT-11 version (SND-2 by the Navy) with a special snub nose to accommodate the then revolutionary gunsight. It carried a pilot and three students

**Left** This B-25's single nose-mounted machine gun may not appear to offer much defence, but this North American twin has eleven more! One especially devastating tactic used in the Pacific in World War 2 was to face the upper turret forwards, thus providing—with port and starboard package guns—a total of seven machine guns. The effect was often literally to cut Japanese ships in two. Access to the nose gun position was via a tunnel, below and to port of the captain and copilot

**Above** This B-25 nose art smacks of a crew coming from down Mexico way. Nose art developed in World War 2, usually revolving around either the fair sex or aggression

**Overleaf** B-25 Mitchells saw much active service with the RAF during the World War 2, as typified by this finely restored example as it taxies out at Tico. Although puny by today's standards, the B-25's 3000-pound bomb load was dropped with lethal effect in just about every theatre in World War 2. This type's most daring escapade was probably General Doolittle's carrier-based attack on Tokyo

**Above** With three of its total of no less than 12 machine guns visible, a B-25J takes off from the VAC runway during the 1989 display. With a crew of five, this 35,000-pound twin has a maximum speed of 272 mph at 13,000 feet and can reach 24,200 feet. One restored B-25, *Georgia Girl*, has a typically colourful background. Bought a few years ago at an auction in Chicago, it had previously been on the Canadian register and confiscated for drug smuggling. It flies today in Air National Guard livery

*Chapter XI* is owned and operated by a group of enthusiasts headed by ex-airline captain 'Robbie' Robinson and Dale Krebsbach, President of Gateway Aviation, and the FBO situated at Tico. They are both in command during this sunset sortie. Almost totally dilapidated when Robbie and his friend found it, this B-25J has been completely rebuilt and still has only 4000 hours total airframe time. Inside, the roar from its two Wright R-2600–982 14-cylinder radials, each producing 1700 hp, calls for any passengers to wear ear defenders. Normal conversation is impossible

# VAC transports

**Left** Two Tico 'Gooneys'—the one in the foreground having been acquired from the Norwegian Air Force and ferried back by VAC stalwarts. Not only do these two C-47s participate in the Valiant Air Command shows, but also—free of charge—take keen lensmen on air-to-air photographic sessions. At the opening of the VAC flying display each day, they also re-enact one of their myriad wartime roles by disgorging parachutists

**Below** 'Pull me back down before take-off fellas!' So crowded is the Tico flight-line that a taxi look-out sitting in the roof hatch of this C-47 makes a lot of sense. The Stars and Stripes? So who says patriotism is dead! Long live Uncle Sam—*McDonald's* and all

**Above** At least some of us know that 'Gooney Bird' refers to this enthusiast's aircraft, the venerable C-47. Or does it, one wonders? Maybe he'll turn around and we can find out!

**Right** There are still over 200 DC-3s and C-47s flying just about all over the world. It was even made under licence in Russia. There cannot be many roles it has not fulfilled, but perhaps one of its most dramatic was that of gunship in Vietnam. 'Spooky', as these AC-47Ds were known, had a simple but effective weapons fit of three 6000 rounds-per-minute SUU-11/A Minigun pods with 54,000 rounds of 7·62 mm ammunition. Airmen in the cabin loaded the guns and cleared away the spent cartridges. Hand-dropped flares were carried for target illumination

**Left** A Fairchild C-119, appropriately named *Georgia Box*, arrives at Tico after flying from Tucson, via Atlanta. The last leg took a respectable two and a half hours with the C-119's normal 160 knot cruising speed boosted by a ten knot tailwind. Developed from the Fairchild C-82, the high-wing, twin-boom, podded fuselage layout gives ease of access to the capacious cargo bay, along with a low sill height. Dave Brady, *Georgia Box*'s owner, acquired the freighter in early 1989. It has around 14,000 hours on the airframe and the two P & W 3350 hp radials—which burn 200 gallons per hour—each has 1000 hours since rebuild

**Left** Have cars (in aeroplane) will travel! As the rear cargo doors open on Dave Brady's Fairchild C-119, first his 'compact' emerges—then his Mercedes! This has to be the ultimate way to visit an airshow. Found at Davis-Monthan Air Force Base as long ago as 1972, it then went to Alaska where it hauled fish. In 1985 it was in private ownership in Tucson, where Dave Brady bought it. To date he has spent more than $30,000 on restoration, especially the control surfaces (none of which are boosted) which were in bad shape

Both inboard and outboard flaps are of modest proportions on the C-119, but ailerons are wide-span, giving this otherwise cumbersome freighter good roll characteristics. 'It turns real good', says owner Dave Brady, another characteristic essential for manoeuvring close to the ground at slow speeds during supply drops, For this, and paradrops, the rear clam-shell doors are removed. The C-82 and C-119 family of Fairchild work-horses has seen many interesting developments, including the installation of a jet engine atop the fuselage to improve 'hot and high' performance at take-off, and even one experimental version with two sets of tandem main undercarriage gears each side, allowing the aircraft—with, in this instance, just an embryonic fuselage—to straddle a container, strap in and fly off

U. S. ARMY PT-22
AIR CORPS SERIAL
NO. AC41-20798
CREW WEIGHT 380 LBS.
SERVICE THIS AIRPLANE
WITH 73 OCTANE FUEL ONLY.
IF NOT AVAILABLE THE NEXT
HIGHER GRADE WILL BE
USED IR EMERGENCY.

# From Recruit to Pursuit

**Left** If you took a friend along in this US Army PT-22, they—and you—had to be weightwatchers! And 78 octane fuel? You can't beat many cars away from the traffic lights with that in your tank!

**Below** The Ryan PT-22 Recruit was the final version of the first low-wing primary trainer—PT-16—to be adopted by the US Army Air Corps in 1939. It was the culmination of a series of trainers that began with the 1934 Ryan ST Sport. Advanced for its time, the ST-22 featured fairly questionable disc brakes and a steerable tailwheel that was best left disconnected

This immaculate PT-22 is powered with a Kinner five-cylinder radial with its own distinctive sound. The earlier and less numerous PT-16 had a Menasco powerplant and both swang wooden two-bladed propellers. Used mainly in civilian contract flying schools, a total of 1048 PT-22s were built until 1943

**Left** A rare bird indeed, the Lockheed
P-38 Lightning was built in ten
versions, totalling 9422 units. But
now they are as difficult to find as
chickens' teeth. This is John
Silberman's renovated example; at
least five more are known to be in
restoration. A truly versatile fighter,
the P-38 was dubbed by the Germans
*Der Gabelschwanz Teufel*—the 'Fork-
tailed Devil'

**Below** With its ultra-slim fuselage
pod, the P-38's cockpit is extremely
roomy by any standards. All controls
are logically grouped and easily
accessible. The P-38M was a two-
seater night fighter version with the
'passenger' partially buried behind
the pilot. The result of a specification
issued in 1937 for a high-altitude
fighter, the Lightning was originally
known as the Lockheed 22, the
company's first combat aircraft. It
first flew as the XP-38 in January
1939

**Above** The VAC Lightning 'cleans up' with its huge single main wheels retracting backwards into the tailbooms. Those booms are not only useful things to nail tailplanes and fins onto, but also house the Allison V-1710–89/91 powerplants (1425 hp each), radiators and oil coolers. Able to fly at 414 mph at 25,000 feet, and with a very useful range of 2260 miles, the Lockheed Lightning typically carried a 20 mm cannon and four 12·7 mm machine guns. It could carry two 500, 1000 or 1600-pound bombs or ten five-inch rockets

**Right** This shark certainly has many teeth—plus an eye or two for an enemy. Curtiss P-40 cowlings were ideal for such artistry and there is no doubt that during a low-level attack the sight and sound of a Warhawk with its teeth bared did little for the bad guy's digestion!

**Above** The roomy 'office' of a Curtis P-40 Warhawk. It even has convenient stowage for the 'bone dome' that no well-dressed P-40 'jockey' would be seen without. The control column is tethered so as to stop the elevator and ailerons waving around in the breeze

**Right** The P-40 was a potent enough beast which could proceed at 378 mph behind the 1360 hp of its Allison V-1710–81/99/115 in-line engine. It carried six 0·50 calibre machine guns in the wings and a 500-pound bomb where this one sports a long-range fuel tank, thus augmenting the Warhawk's normal 240 mile operational radius. An early product of the US War Machine, the P-40 in its almost definitive form (the XP-40 protoype was a converted P-36A) flew in October 1939 and was used in service in low-level and ground attack roles. Under Lease-Lend, P-40s were delivered to both the USSR and China, as well as Britain

**Left** Even at dusk the P-51 looks the picture of elegance. Probably the best known of all US-built fighters, it was initially roughed out on the back of an envelope in a London hotel specifically to meet an RAF requirement from 1940. It is claimed that 48 per cent of all enemy aircraft destroyed in World War 2 were accounted for by P-51s

**Above right** After the Mk 1 P-51 Mustang entered service, Malcolm hoods were introduced to improve visibility. The P-51D had a beautiful bubble canopy, but these did not appear in Europe in significant numbers until the summer of 1944. Several fly with a second seat behind the pilot and some even have dual controls—a great boon for training future private-owner P-51 jockeys, for like most high performance aircraft, it can bite the unwary

**Below right** This is *Stiletto*, a special Reno racer P-51 at Tico. Her rear end looks very much like that of a regular Mustang, but there the similarity stops. Note the tiny faired-in canopy, with just enough visibility and compare the prop with a warbird cousin's. Its diameter is less and it revs a lot faster, being turned by a highly tweaked Merlin drinking a 'special brew'!

**Below** Apart from the vastly different canopy, *Stiletto*'s wings have been cropped to save weight and reduce drag. This 'mod' makes for a longer, faster take-off run and more concrete is needed for landing. But when you want to tank around at over 400 mph, this is how to do it!

**Right** The lovely crackle of mighty Merlins as a row of North American P-51 Mustangs zig-zag along the taxiway towards the take-off point. This manoeuvre was essential in all long-nosed taildraggers as a means of seeing ahead during ground movements. Unlike the Spitfire, the Mustang sported a widely spaced inward retracting undercarriage, much appreciated amongst pilots, especially during cross-wing take-offs and landings

**Inset** Hamilton Standard, who have been making props almost since Wilbur and Orville, are the suppliers for most P-51s, as this example shows. Power behind it is a Packard V-1650–3 Merlin of 1450 hp. The original Mk 1 North American Mustang had the lower-powered Allison V-1710 unit, which was a superb, smooth-running engine, but lacked the two-stage supercharger (and therefore the high-altitude performance) of the V-1650 Merlin

**Above** *Passion Waggon*, a frequent visitor to warbird shows all over the States, poses over the Florida countryside, complete with ecstatic passenger! A beauty like this—the Mustang, not the passenger—is worth in the region of 400,000 dollars. With spares becoming increasingly scarce, several companies now offer newly manufactured parts. Even after the type had been withdrawn from Allied service, it remained on the payroll in Latin America with the air forces of Bolivia, Dominica (the last to retire it in May 1984), Guatamala, Haiti and Nicaragua. Most of the Dominican Mustangs originally served with the Swedish Air Force

**Left** This P-51 sports 'D Day' invasion stripes under its rear fuselage, accentuated by the deep radiator scoop. Used in Europe by the USAF as long-range, high-altitude escort fighters, they were flown by the RAF mainly on low-level offensive sweeps. *Reichsmarschal* Hermann Goering, boss man of the *Luftwaffe*, is claimed to have said that when he saw Mustangs over Berlin, he knew that the war was lost!

Edgar Schmued designed the Mustang and the prototype was built just 102 days after the contract was signed! Its first flight was on 26 October 1940 and until production ceased in 1946, 15,576 had been built—7966 being the popular 'D' version. Performance was impressive: a speed of 437 mph, at 25,000 feet; service ceiling of 41,900 feet and an initial climb rate of 3475 feet/min. Little did Mr Schmued think that his brainchild would still be in the hands of private flyers 50 years after he put pencil to drawing board

# VAC people

**Left** Known as the 'Warthog' by its pilots, the Fairchild A-10 Thunderbolt II is a powerful tank-buster with a startling performance. A pair fly at Tico as part of an impressive US Air Force/Navy display. Built to survive, the A-10 is strong, well-armoured and has as its main armament an awesome seven-barrel Avenger 30 mm rotating cannon in its nose. From its nearly two-and-a-half metre long barrel emerge either 2100 or 4200 rounds a minute

**Below** Bill Noriega, an Air traffic Controller from Miami, is not only the VAC 'air boss'—here he is controlling the flying display with split-second precision from his lofty perch—but now overall Air Show Director. His morning briefings are professional, to the point, and a feast of quick-fire wit

**Left** VAC pilots come in all shapes and sizes, young and old. They all suffer the one disease for which there is no known cure—aviation. Here a group spins a yarn or two in the briefing tent—Bill Noriega's palace. Here, Bill outlines just what will happen to dozens of aircraft, many with totally differing performances, in the sky at the same time. Take-off patterns, display manoeuvres, 'retrievals', emergency procedures and much more. All of which has gone to make Tico and the VAC that bit special

**Above** Avenger pilot 'Coke' Stewart, a man who actually gave up flying for 19 years, sports his straw hat trademark complete with orange windsock. One of Coke's companions appears to be knitting a junior flying jacket—on the principle that it's never too early to fly a warbird

A group of VAC stalwarts dressed as old-timers pose in front of the deceptively large Douglas Skyraider. Their tin-hatted lensman used a Box Brownie, of course, and they all said *'Bully beef and bloody biscuits.'* Cheese was, at least on one side of the Atlantic, rationed

**Left** Tico from the air with not all aircraft yet arrived. In the distance is Cape Canaveral, and Gateway Aviation, Tico's FBO, is top right. Most of the surrounding countryside is flat, with the airfield just above mean sea-level. This makes for excellent spectator viewing. Just visible on the show site are the many amenity stores and snack bars—your every need is taken care of, down to the last 'Portaloo'

**Above** Not only a pretty face, but an effective Military Police-person. She did wonders for recruiting and appears to be about to swot either a miscreant fly or maybe the apprehended villain!

**Overleaf** There's no smoke without fire at Tico, as this dramatic napalm 'pyro' shows. The realism with which the ground-based experts devise the deadly results of bombing and strafing is truly remarkable, as are the noise and heat produced. But it still takes an awful lot of B-25 bomb loads to destroy the toughest of Japanese-held chipboard bridges!